ADAPTED TO SURVIVE

ANIMALS THAT HIDE

Angela Royston

raintree

a Capstone company — publishers for children

Raintree is an imprint of Capstone Global Library Limited, a company incorporated in England and Wales having its registered office at 7 Pilgrim Street, London, EC4V 6LB – Registered company number: 6695582

www.raintreepublishers.co.uk
myorders@raintreepublishers.co.uk

Edited by Dan Nunn, Rebecca Rissman, and Helen Cox Cannons
Designed by Joanna Hinton-Malivoire
Picture research by Mica Brancic
Originated by Capstone Global Library Ltd
Production by Helen McCreath
Printed and bound in China

ISBN 978 1 406 27086 0 (hardback)
17 16 15 14 13
10 9 8 7 6 5 4 3 2 1

ISBN 978 1 406 270938 (paperback)
18 17 16 15 14
10 9 8 7 6 5 4 3 2 1

British Library Cataloguing in Publication Data
A full catalogue record for this book is available from the British Library.

Acknowledgements
We would like to thank the following for permission to reproduce photographs: Alamy p. 27 (© Robert Canis); FLPA pp. 12 (Chris Mattison), 13 (Minden Pictures/sierra Madre/© Patricio Robles Gil); Naturepl.com pp. 6 (© Charlie Summers), 7 (© Kim Taylor), 9 (© Premaphotos), 11 (© Steven Kazlowski), 15 (© Sharon Heald), 19, 22 (© Doug Perrine), 21 (© Wild Wonders of Europe/O. Haar), 23 (© Edwin Giesbers), 25, 29 bottom right (© John Cancalosi), 26 (© Robert Thompson); Shutterstock pp. 14 (© Sally Wallis), 16, 29 top left (© TheRocky41), 17 (© Gary C. Tognoni), 20 (© outdoorsman), 29 bottom left (© Eric Isselee), 29 top right (© Eugene Sim); SuperStock pp. 4 (Bruce & Jan Lichtenberger), 5, 24 (Minden Pictures), 8 (Science Faction/Steven Kazlowski), 10 (FogStock LLC), 18 (Biosphoto).

Cover photograph of a variable lizard reproduced with permission of Shutterstock (© vicspacewalker).

We would like to thank Michael Bright with his invaluable help in the preparation of this book.

Every effort has been made to contact copyright holders of material reproduced in this book. Any omissions will be rectified in subsequent printings if notice is given to the publisher.

Disclaimer
All the internet addresses (URLs) given in this book were valid at the time of going to press. However, due to the dynamic nature of the internet, some addresses may have changed, or sites may have changed or ceased to exist since publication. While the author and publisher regret any inconvenience this may cause readers, no responsibility for any such changes can be accepted by either the author or the publisher.

Some words are shown in bold, **like this.** You can find out what they mean by looking in the glossary.

CONTENTS

GOOD AT HIDING

Many animals are good at hiding. Mice crawl through tiny gaps, crabs shelter under stones on the seashore, and frightened rabbits run into their **burrows**. However, some animals hide by staying still and blending in with the background. This is called **camouflage**.

Hide and seek
How and why
do animals use
camouflage to hide?

WHY DO ANIMALS HIDE?

Hiding helps an animal to **survive**. **Camouflage** gives an extra advantage. It allows an animal to see other animals, without being seen by them! Both **predators** and **prey** use camouflage. A toad, for example, hides from birds and other predators, but it also hides from the insects it eats!

leopard

ADAPTED TO HIDE

An **adaptation** is something special about an animal's body that helps it to **survive**. **Camouflage** is an adaptation, because the animal's skin, fur, or feathers are the same colouring as the background or **habitat**.

ptarmigan

This blue shined grasshopper is so well camouflaged it is almost impossible to see – until it moves!

POLAR BEARS

Polar bears and other Arctic animals have white fur to **camouflage** them against the ice and snow. Polar bears hunt for seals on the ice. They wait quietly until a seal comes above water to breathe. By the time the seal sees the bear, it is too late!

This polar bear is watching a hole in the ice. He is waiting for a seal to appear.

DESERT DISGUISE

Sidewinder snakes live in hot deserts. Their **scaly** skin is pink, orange, grey, or beige to match the sand where they live. Sidewinders hunt at night. During the day, they hide beneath the sand.

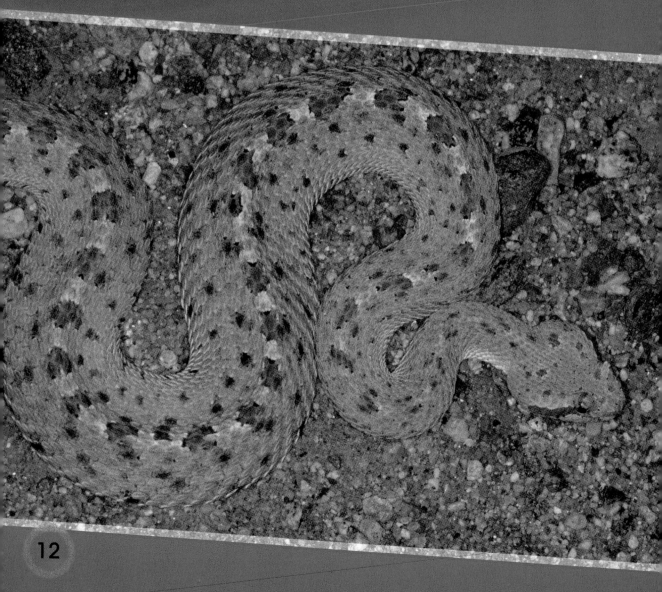

DID YOU KNOW?
Some sidewinders have short, scaly horns above each eye. These horns protect their eyes from sand when they are buried.

TIGER STRIPES

Tigers have orange and white fur with black stripes. They are easy to recognize, but the stripes **camouflage** them in the tropical forests where they live. A tiger hides in the **undergrowth** and waits for **prey**. Then it creeps up until it is near enough to pounce!

15

ZEBRA STRIPES

A zebra's black and white stripes do not blend in with the **grasslands** where they live! However, a zebra's stripes protect it from **predators**. Zebras live together in herds. The stripes make it hard for the predator to pick out one zebra from the rest.

When a predator attacks, the herd runs away.

SHARKS

When a shark is seen from above, its dark back blends in with the dark sea below it.

Like many **predators**, sharks do not want to be spotted before they attack. Their dark backs and light bellies help to hide them from **prey** above and below.

When a shark is seen from below, its light belly is **camouflaged** against the sky.

ARCTIC FOXES

Arctic foxes change colour with the seasons. As summer comes and the snow melts, their white winter fur changes to brown or grey to blend with the rocks. In autumn, their white fur grows back.

It takes several weeks for an Arctic fox to change colour.

QUICK CHANGE

Some animals can change colour very quickly. Types of flatfish and cuttlefish hide from **predators** by changing their skin patterns to match the sand or stones below them. Some chameleons change colour to **camouflage** themselves. They also change colour when they are angry, scared, or to warm up or cool down.

eye

DID YOU KNOW?
It takes this eyed flounder between 2 and 8 seconds to change colour.

flounder

chameleon

PLANTS OR INSECTS?

Some insects disguise themselves as parts of plants! Some look like leaves and others like twigs. They keep very still so that **predators** do not see them. Leaf insects are the same colour as leaves, and they are shaped like leaves, too.

leaf insect

Ouch!
Thorn insects are
shaped just like thorns!

LOOKING FIERCE

Some insects use **camouflage** to stay safe by looking more dangerous. For example, when a bird attacks an elephant hawkmoth caterpillar, it is in for a surprise. The caterpillar pulls its head into its body to look like a snake with a large head and black eye patches!

elephant hawkmoth caterpillar

eye patches

ANIMAL CHALLENGE

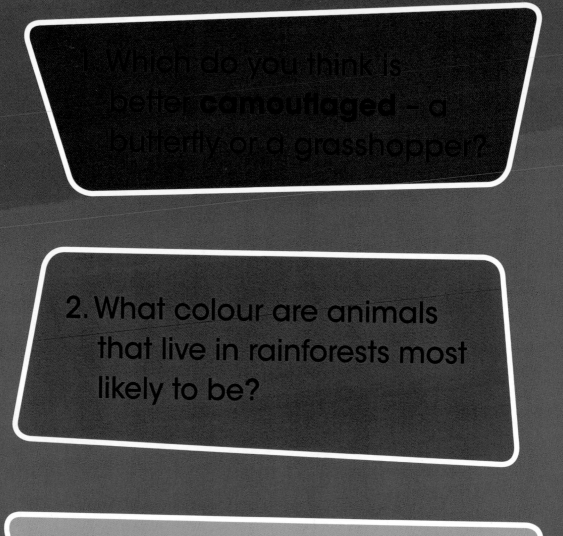

1. Which do you think is better **camouflaged** – a butterfly or a grasshopper?

2. What colour are animals that live in rainforests most likely to be?

3. Why do you think that many animals that live in **grasslands** are brown, not green?

Invent your own camouflaged animal. First, decide what type of **habitat** it lives in and then decide how you will help it to hide. You can use the **adaptations** shown in the photos, or you can make up your own.

stripes

special skills

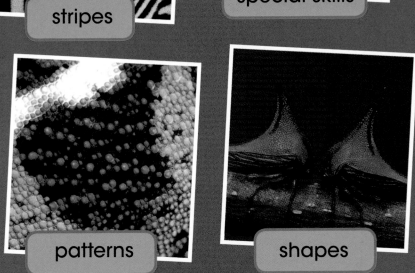

patterns

shapes

Answers to Animal Challenge

1. A grasshopper is well camouflaged against green plants, but most butterflies are not camouflaged.

2. Most rainforest animals are green or brown, like the leaves on the trees.

3. Dry grass is yellow or brown, so animals that live on dry grasslands are usually brown.

GLOSSARY

adaptation special thing about an animal's body that helps it to survive in a particular way or in a particular habitat

burrow home dug below the surface of the ground by some types of animal

camouflage hide by blending in with the background or habitat

grassland area where the main plants are grass and there are few trees

habitat type of environment or landscape where an animal usually lives

predator animal that hunts and kills other animals for food

prey animal that is hunted and eaten by another animal

scaly covered with small, hard plates of skin

survive manage to go on living

undergrowth thick bushes and plants that grow beneath the trees in a forest

FIND OUT MORE

BOOKS

Animal (Dorling Kindersley, 2011)

Animal Encyclopedia (Dorling Kindersley, 2008)

Hidden in the Trees, Barbara Taylor (QED, 2011)

WEBSITES

kids.nationalgeographic.co.uk/kids/animals/creaturefeature
Click on particular animals, such as sharks or polar bears, to find out more about them.

www.abc.net.au/beasts/playground/camouflage.htm
Play the camouflage game on this website and test if you have picked the best camouflage to match different backgrounds.

www.bbc.co.uk/nature/adaptations/camouflage
This BBC website has several short videos showing particular examples of camouflage, including mountain hares, flounders, and cuttlefish.

www.ypte.org.uk/animal-facts.php
Find out more about many different animals on this website.

INDEX